WAR PLANES

Strike Fighters:
The F/A-18E/F Super Hornets
by Bill Sweetman

DISCARD

CAPSTONE
HIGH-INTEREST
BOOKS

an imprint of Capstone Press
Mankato, Minnesota

Capstone High-Interest Books are published by Capstone Press
151 Good Counsel Drive, P.O. Box 669, Mankato, Minnesota 56002
http://www.capstone-press.com

Library of Congress Cataloging-in-Publication Data
Sweetman, Bill.
    Strike fighters: the F/A-18E/F Super Hornets/By Bill Sweetman.
    p. cm.—(War planes)
    Includes bibliographical references and index.
    Summary: Introduces the F-18 Super Hornets, their missions, equipment,
weapons, and use in the military.
    ISBN 0-7368-1070-6
    1. Hornet (Jet fighter plane)—Juvenile literature. [1. Hornet (Jet fighter
plane)] I. Title. II. War planes.
UG1242.F5 S962 2002
623.7'464—dc21   2001003638

**Special thanks to the members of the U.S. Navy's F/A-18 Program Team for
their help in preparing this book.**

Editorial Credits
Matt Doeden, editor; Timothy Halldin, cover designer, interior layout
    designer, and interior illustrator; Katy Kudela, photo researcher

Photo Credits
Boeing Management Company, 23
Ted Carlson/Fotodynamics, 9, 10, 13, 16–17, 18, 24, 27, 28
U.S. Navy photo, cover, 1, 4, 6, 21

1 2 3 4 5 6 07 06 05 04 03 02

Table of Contents

Chapter One

Learn About

- Carrier takeoff
- The Super Hornet's mission
- Differences from the Hornet

The Super Hornet in Action

The aircraft carrier USS *Abraham Lincoln* moves through the water at 25 miles (40 kilometers) per hour. A gray Super Hornet fighter plane moves slowly on the front of the ship's huge deck.

Crew members hook a steel launch bar to the plane's front right wheel. The other end of the bar rests in a long slot in the deck. Steam hisses from the slot.

The Super Hornet is the Navy's best carrier aircraft.

The pilot brings the plane's engines to full power. But the plane does not move. A second steel bar on the plane's rear holds it to the deck. This bar is called the holdback bar. Behind the plane, large steel panels tilt up. This blast deflector forces the jet engine's exhaust gases up and away from the deck.

The carrier's cat officer is in charge of the plane's launch. The pilot salutes to signal that he is ready to take off. The cat officer makes sure everything is ready. He then points two fingers straight down toward the deck. This signal begins the launch of the plane.

Another crew member called the catapult operator flips a switch. Steam from the aircraft carrier's engines bursts into the catapult. The catapult pulls on the launch bar. The holdback bar unlatches. The Super Hornet rockets forward. It reaches a speed of more than 150 miles (241 kilometers) per hour in two seconds. The plane quickly climbs into the air. The pilot is ready to begin his mission.

About the Super Hornet

The F/A-18E/F Super Hornet is a carrier aircraft. It can take off from and land on aircraft carriers. The Super Hornet is the U.S. Navy's best and newest carrier aircraft.

The Super Hornet is a large, powerful strike fighter. It carries bombs, missiles, and guns. Pilots can use Super Hornets to attack ground targets, enemy ships, or other aircraft. Pilots also can use Super Hornets as bomber planes.

The U.S. Navy began using the Super Hornet in 1995. Today, the Navy uses two models of the airplane. The Boeing Company builds both models. The E model has only one seat. The F model includes a second seat behind the pilot.

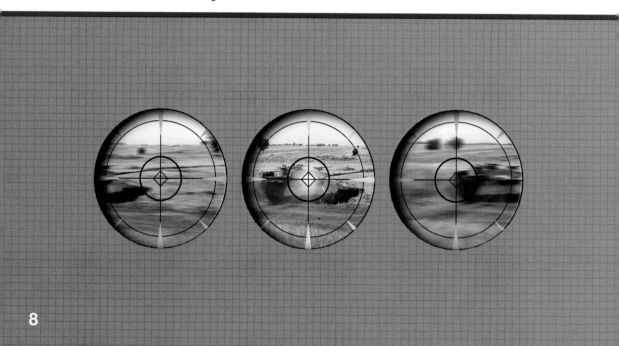

The Super Hornet is a large, powerful strike fighter.

The Super Hornet is based on earlier designs of the F/A-18 Hornet. The Navy first used this aircraft in 1983. The Hornet was an important fighter plane during the Gulf War (1991).

The Super Hornet is bigger than the Hornet. It has larger wings and more powerful engines. The Super Hornet also can carry more weapons and fuel than the Hornet. The Super Hornet even can refuel other planes during flight.

Chapter Two

Learn About

- Body design
- Engine power
- Head-up display (HUD)

Inside the Super Hornet

The Super Hornet is a large fighter plane. It is 60 feet, 3 inches (18.5 meters) long. It has broad, straight wings. The Super Hornet has two rear wings called horizontal stabilators. The stabilators help the pilot control the plane at high speeds. The Super Hornet also has two vertical rudders attached to the plane's rear. The rudders help the pilot make tight turns. They also help the pilot control the plane's nose when it is pointing up.

Landing and Takeoff Equipment

The Super Hornet needs special equipment to take off from and land on aircraft carriers. Carrier landings are especially difficult for pilots. Wind and waves can make landing a challenge. Super Hornets do not have enough room to stop normally on a carrier deck. They need extra help to stop in time.

A Super Hornet pilot flies straight toward the carrier deck to land. A hook on the plane's tail must connect with a steel cable stretched across the carrier deck. This cable is called an arrester wire. The arrester wire pulls against the hook. This action quickly slows down the plane. The plane's front wheels then slam into the deck. The Super Hornet comes to a full stop in less than two seconds.

Carrier takeoffs also require special equipment. Carrier decks are too short for standard takeoffs. Super Hornets have launch bars that attach to catapults. The catapults use power from the carrier's steam engines to pull planes quickly up to flying speed. Planes could not take off from carriers without this extra speed.

Strong landing gear helps Super Hornets stop quickly.

Engines

The Super Hornet is powered by two jet engines. Each engine provides 22,000 pounds (9,977 kilograms) of thrust. This force pushes the airplane through the air. The Super Hornet's powerful engines allow it to reach speeds of more than 1,300 miles (2,100 kilometers) per hour.

A square jet inlet lies under each of the Super Hornet's main wings. Air enters through these openings and passes through the engines. The engines heat the air to provide the plane's thrust.

Pilot Controls

The Super Hornet has many controls and gauges inside its cockpit. Pilots use the controls to fly the planes. Pilots use gauges to keep track of the planes' speed, location, and weapons.

The Super Hornet's main controls are the control stick and the throttle. Pilots steer their planes with the control stick. They also can use it to fire some weapons. Pilots control their planes' speed with the throttle. Many controls and buttons are located on the stick and throttle. Pilots use these controls to operate

F/A-18E/F Specifications

Function:	Multi-role attack and fighter aircraft
Manufacturer:	Boeing (formerly McDonnell Douglas)
Date Deployed:	December 1995
Length:	60 feet, 3 inches (18.5 meters)
Wingspan:	44 feet, 9 inches (13.7 meters)
Height:	16 feet (4.9 meters)
Max. Weight:	66,000 pounds (29,932 kilograms)
Payload:	17,750 pounds (8,032 kilograms)
Engine:	Two F414-GE-400 turbofan engines
Thrust:	22,000 pounds (9,977 kilograms) per engine
Speed:	1,300 miles (2,100 kilometers) per hour
Ceiling:	50,000 feet (15,240 meters)
Combat Range:	1,465 miles (2,358 kilometers)

Super Hornet systems without removing their hands from the stick or throttle.

Most of the Super Hornet's gauges are in the front of the cockpit. The pilot uses a head-up display (HUD) to read gauges. The pilot can look at the HUD without looking down. All the necessary flight information is available to the pilot in one place.

rudder

stabilator

rear landing gear

The F/A-18F Super Hornet

cockpit

VFA-122

101

center line tank

front landing gear

Chapter Three

Learn About

- Sidewinder missiles
- Laser-guided bombs
- Defensive weapons

Weapons and Tactics

The Super Hornet carries a variety of weapons to help pilots complete missions. The weight of a Super Hornet's weapons and equipment is called the payload. Pilots use machine guns, missiles, and bombs to attack ground targets and enemy aircraft. The number and kinds of weapons a Super Hornet carries depend on the pilot's mission.

Guns and Air-to-Air Missiles

All Super Hornets carry a six-barrel M61 machine gun in the plane's nose. This gun can fire 100 bullets per second. Pilots use machine guns mainly against enemy aircraft.

The Super Hornet often carries air-to-air missiles for combat with other aircraft. The AIM-9 Sidewinder is one common missile. The Super Hornet carries Sidewinders on the tips of its wings. The Sidewinder is effective in close combat. It includes a heat-seeking device in its nose. This equipment guides the Sidewinder toward sources of heat such as the exhaust from enemy planes.

The Super Hornet also may carry the AIM-120 AMRAAM. AMRAAM is short for "Advanced Medium-Range Air-to-Air Missile." Pilots often call these missiles "Slammers." The AMRAAM includes a built-in radar system that uses radio waves to locate targets.

Navy members load bullets for the F/A-18's guns.

Surface Weapons

Super Hornet pilots sometimes attack enemy ships. The Super Hornet carries a missile called a Harpoon for these missions. The Harpoon missile is powered by a small jet engine. The Harpoon has a large warhead that explodes when the missile hits its target.

The SLAM (Stand-off Land Attack Missile) is a version of the Harpoon. Pilots use the SLAM against targets on land. The SLAM includes a camera and a radio control link. The missile sends a picture through the radio control link. The pilot can use this picture to choose the exact spot for the missile to strike.

Laser-guided bombs (LGBs) are another surface weapon. Super Hornet pilots aim a narrow beam of light called a laser beam at a target. They then release the LGBs. The LGBs have sensors that detect the laser. The bombs then fly toward the target.

Defensive Weapons

Some Super Hornet weapons are designed to protect the plane from enemy missiles. Enemies may use surface-to-air missiles (SAMs) to destroy Super Hornets.

The Super Hornet carries a variety of missiles.

The Super Hornet may carry the AGM-88 HARM (High-Speed Anti-Radiation Missile). The AGM-88 can detect the signals that guide SAMs. It uses these signals to intercept the SAMs. The AGM-88 destroys the SAMs before the missiles can reach their targets.

The AGM-154 Joint Stand-Off Weapon (JSOW) is another defensive weapon. The JSOW is a gliding weapon. It has no engine. The JSOW glides to its target and releases 145 small bombs. These bombs can destroy enemy missile launchers and other targets.

Chapter Four

Learn About

- Towed decoys
- Radar jamming
- Future plans

The Future

The Super Hornet is one of the U.S. Navy's newest and most effective airplanes. Navy officials are pleased with the Super Hornet's performance. But they also know that the plane can be better. The Navy has already made some improvements to the Super Hornet. These improvements help the Super Hornet remain one of the best and most modern planes in service.

New Defenses

New Super Hornets may carry a new device to protect it from SAMs. This device is called a towed decoy. The decoy is a small dart on the end of a long cable. The cable is attached to the plane's rear. The dart sends out electronic signals designed to confuse SAM radar. SAM radar may see the dart and the plane as a single target. SAMs then would be aimed at the center of the combined target. These missiles would miss the Super Hornet.

The Navy may buy a special version of the Super Hornet to attack enemy radar stations. These Super Hornets will carry electronic devices to help pilots detect enemy radar. Pilots then will be able to aim powerful radio signals at enemy radar stations. These signals prevent radar from working properly. This action is called "jamming." Enemy troops at radar stations would not be able to use radar to aim missiles. Radar jamming would keep Super Hornet pilots safe from SAM attacks.

New systems help pilots stay safe during missions.

The Navy may buy as many as 1,000 F/A-18s by 2012.

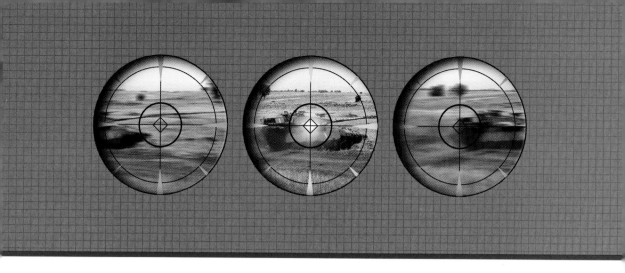

Future Usefulness

The Navy buys 48 new Super Hornets each year. It plans to buy at least 500 Super Hornets by the year 2012. But some military experts believe the Navy will buy as many as 1,000 Super Hornets.

The Navy has no plans to replace the Super Hornet in the near future. New computers, radar devices, and weapons will keep the Super Hornet up to date. The Navy also may add more new systems such as radar jamming equipment.

The Super Hornet is fast and powerful. It can make quick turns. It can carry a variety of weapons. No other U.S. military aircraft can perform many of the Super Hornet's missions. The Super Hornet will remain an important part of the military for many years to come.

Words to Know

arrester wire (uh-REST-uhr WIRE)—a steel cable that is stretched across an aircraft carrier's deck; arrester wires help landing planes stop quickly.

catapult (KAT-uh-puhlt)—a device used to launch airplanes from the deck of an aircraft carrier

intercept (in-tur-SEPT)—to stop the movement of an object

laser beam (LAY-zur BEEM)—a narrow, intense beam of light; some Super Hornets carry bombs that use laser beams to locate targets.

mission (MISH-uhn)—a military task

radar (RAY-dar)—equipment that uses radio waves to locate and guide objects

rudder (RUHD-ur)—a metal plate attached to a plane to help the pilot steer

stabilator (STAY-buh-lay-tuhr)—the rear wing of an airplane

thrust (THRUHST)—the force created by a jet engine; thrust pushes an airplane forward.

To Learn More

Chant, Christopher. *Military Aircraft.* The World's Greatest Aircraft. Philadelphia: Chelsea House, 2000.

Green, Michael. *The United States Navy.* Serving Your Country. Mankato, Minn.: Capstone High-Interest Books, 1998.

Maynard, Christopher. *Aircraft.* The Need for Speed. Minneapolis: Lerner Publications, 1999.

Useful Addresses

Naval Historical Center
Washington Navy Yard
805 Kidder Breese SE
Washington, DC 20374-5060

Navy Public Affairs Center
9420 Third Avenue
Suite 200
Norfolk, VA 23511-2127

Internet Sites

Boeing—F/A-18E/F Super Hornet

http://www.boeing.com/defense-space/
    military/fa18ef/fa18ef.htm

Hornet Hyperlink

http://pma265.navair.navy.mil/hornet.html

The United States Navy

http://www.navy.mil

Index